First hundred ~~ds in~~ ~~sian~~

Amery

~~hen~~ Cartwright

~~tant:~~ Katerina Burgess

and Jan McCafferty

 There is a litt ~~uck~~ to find in every picture.

Гостиная

*ga**stee**naya*　　The living room

папа
***pa**pa*
Daddy

мама
***ma**ma*
Mummy

мальчик
***mal'**chik*
boy

2

девочка
dyevachka
girl

ребёнок
ribyawnak
baby

собака
sabaka
dog

кошка
koshka
cat

Одежда   *adyezhda*   Clothes

обувь
oboof'
shoes

трусы
troosy
pants

джемпер
djempir
jumper

майка
*may*ka
vest

брюки
*bryoo*ki
trousers

футболка
foot*bol*ka
t-shirt

носки
nas*kee*
socks

5

Кухня *kooh*nya   The kitchen

хлеб
hlyep
bread

молоко
*mala**ko***
milk

яйца
yaytsa
eggs

яблоко
yablaka
apple

апельсин
apil'**seen**
orange

банан
ba**nan**
banana

Мытьё посуды

myt'yo pasoody Washing up

стол
stol
table

стул
stool
chair

тарелка
taryelka
plate

8

нож
nosh
knife

вилка
veelka
fork

ложка
loshka
spoon

кружка
krushka
cup

Игрушки　 *igroosh*ki　 Toys

лошадь
*losh*at'
horse

овца
*af***tsa**
sheep

корова
*ka***ro**va
cow

курица
kooritsa
hen

свинья
sveen'ya
pig

поезд
poyest
train

кубики
koobiki
blocks

В гостях

v gastiah   On a visit

бабушка
***ba**booshka*
Granny

дедушка
***dye**dooshka*
Grandpa

тапочки
***ta**pachki*
slippers

пальто
pal'to
coat

платье
plat'ye
dress

шапка
shapka
hat

Парк

park   The park

дерево
*de*ryeva
tree

цветок
*tsvye***tok**
flower

качели
*ka***chye***li*
swings

мяч
myach
ball

детская горка
dyetskaya gorka
slide

сапоги
sapagee
boots

птица
pteetsa
bird

лодка
lotka
boat

Улица   *oolitsa*   The street

машина
masheena
car

велосипед
vilasipyet
bicycle

самолёт
samalyot
plane

грузовик
*grooza**veek***
truck

автобус
*af**taw**boos*
bus

дом
dom
house

Вечеринка *vichireenka* The party

воздушный шар
vazdooshniy shar
balloon

торт
tort
cake

часы
chasy
clock

мороженое
*ma**ro**zhenaye*
ice cream

рыба
***ry**ba*
fish

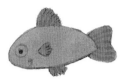

печенье
*pi**chen'**ye*
biscuits

конфеты
*kan**fye**ty*
sweets

Бассейн

*bas**seyn*** The swimming pool

рука
*roo**ka***
arm

кисть руки
keest' *rooki*
hand

нога
*na**ga***
leg

ступня
stoopnya
feet

пальцы ноги
pal'**tsy na**gee
toes

голова
*gala**va***
head

попа
***paw**pa*
bottom

Раздевалка

*razdi**val**ka*   The changing room

рот
rot
mouth

глаза
*gla**za***
eyes

уши
***oo**shi*
ears

нос	волосы	расчёска	щётка
nos	**vo**lasy	ras**chos**ka	**shchyot**ka
nose	hair	comb	brush

23

Магазин   *magazeen*   The shop

красный
krasniy
red

голубой
galooboy
blue

зелёный
zilyoniy
green

24

жёлтый
zholtiy
yellow

розовый
rozaviy
pink

белый
byeliy
white

чёрный
chorniy
black

Ванная комната

*van*naya *kom*nata

The bathroom

мыло
*my*lo
soap

полотенце
pala*tyen*tse
towel

туалет
tooa*lyet*
toilet

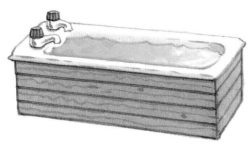

ванна
***van**na*
bath

живот
*zhi**vot***
tummy

утка
***oot**ka*
duck

27

Спальня   *spal'nya*   The bedroom

кровать
kravat'
bed

лампа
lampa
lamp

окно
akno
window

дверь
dver'
door

книга
kneega
book

кукла
kookla
doll

мишка
meeshka
teddy

29

Match the words to the pictures

апельсин

банан

вилка

джемпер

книга

корова

кошка

кукла

лампа

майка

машина

мишка

молоко

мороженое

мяч

нож

носки

окно

поезд

рыба

сапоги

свинья

собака

стол

торт

утка

часы

шапка

яблоко

яйцо

Числа *chees*la Numbers

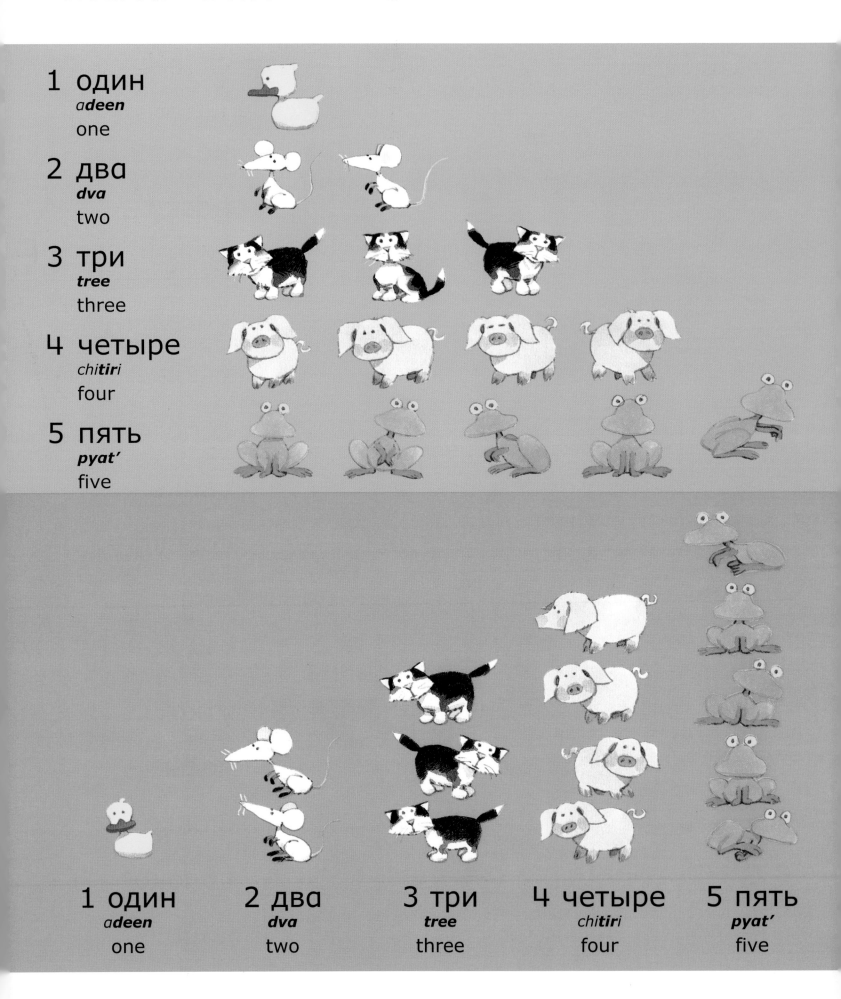

1 один
*a***deen**
one

2 два
dva
two

3 три
tree
three

4 четыре
chitiri
four

5 пять
pyat'
five

1 один
*a***deen**
one

2 два
dva
two

3 три
tree
three

4 четыре
chitiri
four

5 пять
pyat'
five

Saying Russian words

Russian is written in the Cyrillic (say "sirilik") alphabet. This may look strange at first, but it is quite easy to learn. Once you have looked at all the letters, try writing your name in Cyrillic. This is a good way to remember the letters and their sounds. Some Cyrillic letters look like ones in the English alphabet, but sound different: the transcription will help you learn the Russian sounds.

Russian words follow strict rules. In English, you can't always tell how something should sound from the way it is spelled (for example, "ow" sounds different in "cow" and "low"). But in Russian, all you need to know is the sound that the letters make, and where to put the stress. The stress is the part of the word that sounds stronger. English words have this too, like the "day" part of "today". So you know which part to stress, it is written in the book **like this**. The sound of some vowels can change slightly, depending on whether they are stressed or unstressed, so check the transcription carefully.

Vowels

A a   *a* as in *mat*

O o   *aw* as in *paw* when stressed
     ar as in *car* when not stressed

Э э   *e* as in *let*

У у   *oo* as in *pool*

Ы ы   closest sound is the *ei* in *being*. Purse your lips as if you're about to say "O". Keep your tongue in that position, then pull back your lips and start saying "eeee". This letter is normally shown as "y" in the transcriptions.

Я я   *ya* as in *yard*

Е е   *ye* as in *yet*

Ё ё   *yo* as in *yonder*

Ю ю   *yu* sounding like *you*

И и   *ee* as in *feet* when stressed
     i as in *fit* when unstressed

Й й   *y* as in *boy*

Consonants

Б б   *b* as in *book*

В в   *v* as in *van*

Г г   *g* as in *get*

Д д   *d* as in *day*

Ж ж   *zh* like the *s* in *pleasure*

З з   *z* as in *zoo*

К к   *k* as in *kick*

Л л   *l* as in *lamp*

М м   *m* as in *milk*

Н н   *n* as in *net*

П п   *p* as in *pet*

Р р   *r* as in *rock* (rolled *r*)

С с   *s* as in *sit*

Т т   *t* as in *top*

Ф ф   *f* as in *foot*

Х х   *ch* as in Scottish *loch*

Ц ц   *ts* as in *cats*

Ч ч   *ch* as in *cheese*

Ш ш   *sh* as in *shop*

Щ щ   *shch* as in *fresh*

Ъ ъ   "hard sign" (very rare) adds a short pause

Ь ь   "soft sign" shows that the letter before it ends with a soft *y* sound. Shown as ' in the transcription.

Word list

Here are all the Russian words in the book, in Cyrillic alphabetical order. Next to each word you can see how to say it and its meaning in English. To help you find words in the list, the Cyrillic alphabet is given below.

а б в г д е ё ж з и й к л м н о п р с т у ф х ц ч ш щ ъ ы ь э ю я

а
автобус	*af**taw**boos*	bus
апельсин	*apil'**seen***	orange

б
бабушка	***ba**booshka*	Granny
банан	*ba**nan***	banana
бассейн	*bas**seyn***	swimming pool
белый	***bye**liy*	white
брюки	***bryoo**ki*	trousers

в
ванна	***van**na*	bath
ванная комната	***van**naya **kom**nata*	bathroom
велосипед	*vilasi**pyet***	bicycle
вечеринка	*vichi**reen**ka*	party
в гостях	*v gas**tiah***	on a visit
вилка	***veel**ka*	fork
воздушный шар	*vaz**doosh**niy **shar***	balloon
волосы	***vo**lasy*	hair

г
глаза	*gla**za***	eyes
голова	*gala**va***	head
голубой	*galoo**boy***	blue
гостиная	*gas**tee**naya*	living room
грузовик	*grooza**veek***	truck

д
два	***dva***	two
дверь	***dver'***	door
девочка	***dye**vachka*	girl
дедушка	***dye**dooshka*	Grandpa
дерево	***de**ryeva*	tree
детская горка	***dye**tskaya **gor**ka*	slide

джемпер	***djem**pir*	jumper
дом	***dom***	house

ж
жёлтый	***zhol**tiy*	yellow
живот	*zhi**vot***	tummy

з
зелёный	*zi**lyo**niy*	green

и
игрушки	*i**groosh**ki*	toys

к
качели	*ka**chye**li*	swings
кисть руки	***keest'** rooki*	hand
книга	***knee**ga*	book
конфеты	*kan**fye**ty*	sweets
корова	*ka**ro**va*	cow
кошка	***kosh**ka*	cat
красный	***kras**niy*	red
кровать	*kra**vat'***	bed
кружка	***krush**ka*	cup
кубики	***koo**biki*	blocks
кукла	***kook**la*	doll
курица	***koo**ritsa*	hen
кухня	***kooh**nya*	kitchen

л
лампа	***lam**pa*	lamp
лодка	***lot**ka*	boat
ложка	***losh**ka*	spoon
лошадь	***losh**at'*	horse

м
магазин	*maga**zeen***	shop
майка	***may**ka*	vest
мальчик	***mal'**chik*	boy
мама	***ma**ma*	Mummy
машина	*ma**shee**na*	car
мишка	***meesh**ka*	teddy